DEATHS A

ALDINE PAPERBACKS

Volumes in the Aldine Paperbacks now include works by Dylan Thomas, Mrs Robert Henrey, Maurice Wiggin, Constance Spry, Ogden Nash, Brigadier C. N. Barclay, Joseph Conrad, Norbert Casteret, Mary Norton, Kitty Barne, Elizabeth Kendall, W. H. Murray, James Pennethorne Hughes, Rupert Gleadow, Jean Rook, R. S. Rait Kerr, Marie Hartley and Joan Ingilby, etc. etc. A complete list is available from bookseller or publishers on request.

Dylan Thomas

DEATHS and ENTRANCES

J. M. DENT & SONS LTD

Made in Great Britain
at the
Aldine Press · Letchworth · Herts
for
J. M. DENT & SONS LTD
Aldine House · Bedford Street · London
First published 1946
Paperback edition 1968
Reprinted 1971

ISBN: 0 460 02075 7

CONTENTS

The Conversation of Prayer

The conversation of prayers about to be said
By the child going to bed and the man on the stairs
Who climbs to his dying love in her high room,
The one not caring to whom in his sleep he will move
And the other full of tears that she will be dead,

Turns in the dark on the sound they know will arise
Into the answering skies from the green ground,
From the man on the stairs and the child by his bed.
The sound about to be said in the two prayers
For the sleep in a safe land and the love who dies

Will be the same grief flying. Whom shall they calm?
Shall the child sleep unharmed or the man be crying?
The conversation of prayers about to be said
Turns on the quick and the dead, and the man on the stairs
To night shall find no dying but alive and warm

In the fire of his care his love in the high room.
And the child not caring to whom he climbs his prayer
Shall drown in a grief as deep as his true grave,
And mark the dark eyed wave, through the eyes of sleep,
Dragging him up the stairs to one who lies dead.

A Refusal to Mourn the Death, by Fire, of a Child in London

NEVER until the mankind making
Bird beast and flower
Fathering and all humbling darkness
Tells with silence the last light breaking
And the still hour
Is come of the sea tumbling in harness

And I must enter again the round
Zion of the water bead
And the synagogue of the ear of corn
Shall I let pray the shadow of a sound
Or sow my salt seed
In the least valley of sackcloth to mourn

The majesty and burning of the child's death.
I shall not murder
The mankind of her going with a grave truth
Nor blaspheme down the stations of the breath
With any further
Elegy of innocence and youth.

Deep with the first dead lies London's daughter,
Robed in the long friends,
The grains beyond age, the dark veins of her mother,
Secret by the unmourning water
Of the riding Thames.
After the first death, there is no other.

Poem in October

It was my thirtieth year to heaven
Woke to my hearing from harbour and neighbour wood
And the mussel pooled and the heron
Priested shore
The morning beckon
With water praying and call of seagull and rook
And the knock of sailing boats on the net webbed wall
Myself to set foot
That second
In the still sleeping town and set forth.

My birthday began with the water-
Birds and the birds of the winged trees flying my name
Above the farms and the white horses
And I rose
In rainy autumn
And walked abroad in a shower of all my days.
High tide and the heron dived when I took the road
Over the border
And the gates
Of the town closed as the town awoke.

A springful of larks in a rolling
Cloud and the roadside bushes brimming with whistling
Blackbirds and the sun of October
Summery
On the hill's shoulder,
Here were fond climates and sweet singers suddenly

Come in the morning where I wandered and listened
To the rain wringing
Wind blow cold
In the wood faraway under me.

Pale rain over the dwindling harbour
And over the sea wet church the size of a snail
With its horns through mist and the castle
Brown as owls
But all the gardens
Of spring and summer were blooming in the tall tales
Beyond the border and under the lark full cloud.
There could I marvel
My birthday
Away but the weather turned around.

It turned away from the blithe country
And down the other air and the blue altered sky
Streamed again a wonder of summer
With apples
Pears and red currants
And I saw in the turning so clearly a child's
Forgotten mornings when he walked with his mother
Through the parables
Of sun light
And the legends of the green chapels

And the twice told fields of infancy
That his tears burned my cheeks and his heart moved in mine.

These were the woods the river and sea
Where a boy
In the listening
Summertime of the dead whispered the truth of his joy
To the trees and the stones and the fish in the tide.
And the mystery
Sang alive
Still in the water and singingbirds.

And there could I marvel my birthday
Away but the weather turned around. And the true
Joy of the long dead child sang burning
In the sun.
It was my thirtieth
Year to heaven stood there then in the summer noon
Though the town below lay leaved with October blood.
O may my heart's truth
Still be sung
On this high hill in a year's turning.

This Side of the Truth

(for Llewelyn)

THIS side of the truth,
You may not see, my son,
King of your blue eyes
In the blinding country of youth,
That all is undone,
Under the unminding skies,
Of innocence and guilt
Before you move to make
One gesture of the heart or head,
Is gathered and spilt
Into the winding dark
Like the dust of the dead.

Good and bad, two ways
Of moving about your death
By the grinding sea,
King of your heart in the blind days,
Blow away like breath,
Go crying through you and me
And the souls of all men
Into the innocent
Dark, and the guilty dark, and good
Death, and bad death, and then
In the last element
Fly like the stars' blood,

Like the sun's tears,
Like the moon's seed, rubbish
And fire, the flying rant
Of the sky, king of your six years.
And the wicked wish,
Down the beginning of plants
And animals and birds,
Water and light, the earth and sky,
Is cast before you move,
And all your deeds and words,
Each truth, each lie,
Die in unjudging love.

To Others than You

FRIEND by enemy I call you out.

You with a bad coin in your socket,
You my friend there with a winning air
Who palmed the lie on me when you looked
Brassily at my shyest secret,
Enticed with twinkling bits of the eye
Till the sweet tooth of my love bit dry,
Rasped at last, and I stumbled and sucked,
Whom now I conjure to stand as thief
In the memory worked by mirrors,
With unforgettably smiling act,
Quickness of hand in the velvet glove
And my whole heart under your hammer,
Were once such a creature, so gay and frank
A desireless familiar
I never thought to utter or think
While you displaced a truth in the air,

That though I loved them for their faults
As much as for their good,
My friends were enemies on stilts
With their heads in a cunning cloud.

Love in the Asylum

A STRANGER has come
To share my room in the house not right in the head,
A girl mad as birds

Bolting the night of the door with her arm her plume.
Strait in the mazed bed
She deludes the heaven-proof house with entering clouds

Yet she deludes with walking the nightmarish room,
At large as the dead,
Or rides the imagined oceans of the male wards.

She has come possessed
Who admits the delusive light through the bouncing wall,
Possessed by the skies

She sleeps in the narrow trough yet she walks the dust
Yet raves at her will
On the madhouse boards worn thin by my walking tears.

And taken by light in her arms at long and dear last
I may without fail
Suffer the first vision that set fire to the stars.

Unluckily for a Death

UNLUCKILY for a death
Waiting with phoenix under
The pyre yet to be lighted of my sins and days,
And for the woman in shades
Saint carved and sensual among the scudding
Dead and gone, dedicate forever to my self
Though the brawl of the kiss has not occurred,
On the clay cold mouth, on the fire
Branded forehead, that could bind
Her constant, nor the winds of love broken wide
To the wind the choir and cloister
Of the wintry nunnery of the order of lust
Beneath my life, that sighs for the seducer's coming
In the sun strokes of summer,

Loving on this sea banged guilt
My holy lucky body
Under the cloud against love is caught and held and kissed
In the mill of the midst
Of the descending day, the dark our folly,
Cut to the still star in the order of the quick
But blessed by such heroic hosts in your every
Inch and glance that the wound
Is certain god, and the ceremony of souls
Is celebrated there, and communion between suns.
Never shall my self chant
About the saint in shades while the endless breviary
Turns of your prayed flesh, nor shall I shoo the bird below me:
The death biding two lie lonely.

I see the tigron in tears
In the androgynous dark,
His striped and noon maned tribe striding to holocaust,
The she mules bear their minotaurs,
The duck billed platypus broody in a milk of birds.
I see the wanting nun saint carved in a garb
Of shades, symbol of desire beyond my hours
And guilts, great crotch and giant
Continence. I see the unfired phoenix, herald
And heaven crier, arrow now of aspiring
And the renouncing of islands.
All love but for the full assemblage in flower
Of the living flesh is monstrous or immortal,
And the grave its daughters.

Love, my fate got luckily,
Teaches with no telling
That the phoenix' bid for heaven and the desire after
Death in the carved nunnery
Both shall fail if I bow not to your blessing
Nor walk in the cool of your mortal garden
With immortality at my side like Christ the sky.
This I know from the native
Tongue of your translating eyes. The young stars told me,
Hurling into beginning like Christ the child.
Lucklessly she must lie patient
And the vaulting bird be still. O my true love, hold me.
In your every inch and glance is the globe of genesis spun,
And the living earth your sons.

The Hunchback in the Park

THE hunchback in the park
A solitary mister
Propped between trees and water
From the opening of the garden lock
That lets the trees and water enter
Until the Sunday sombre bell at dark

Eating bread from a newspaper
Drinking water from the chained cup
That the children filled with gravel
In the fountain basin where I sailed my ship
Slept at night in a dog kennel
But nobody chained him up.

Like the park birds he came early
Like the water he sat down
And Mister they called Hey mister
The truant boys from the town
Running when he had heard them clearly
On out of sound

Past lake and rockery
Laughing when he shook his paper
Hunchbacked in mockery
Through the loud zoo of the willow groves
Dodging the park keeper
With his stick that picked up leaves.

And the old dog sleeper
Alone between nurses and swans
While the boys among willows
Made the tigers jump out of their eyes
To roar on the rockery stones
And the groves were blue with sailors

Made all day until bell time
A woman figure without fault
Straight as a young elm
Straight and tall from his crooked bones
That she might stand in the night
After the locks and chains

All night in the unmade park
After the railings and shrubberies
The birds the grass the trees the lake
And the wild boys innocent as strawberries
Had followed the hunchback
To his kennel in the dark.

Into her Lying Down Head

(I)

INTO her lying down head
His enemies entered bed,
Under the encumbered eyelid,
Through the rippled drum of the hair-buried ear;
And Noah's rekindled now unkind dove
Flew man-bearing there.
Last night in a raping wave
Whales unreined from the green grave
In fountains of origin gave up their love,
Along her innocence glided
Juan aflame and savagely young King Lear,
Queen Catherine howling bare
And Samson drowned in his hair,
The colossal intimacies of silent
Once seen strangers or shades on a stair;
There the dark blade and wanton sighing her down
To a haycock couch and the scythes of his arms
Rode and whistled a hundred times
Before the crowing morning climbed;
Man was the burning England she was sleep-walking, and the enamouring island
Made her limbs blind by luminous charms,
Sleep to a newborn sleep in a swaddling loin-leaf stroked and sang
And his runaway beloved childlike laid in the acorned sand.

(II)

There where a numberless tongue
Wound their room with a male moan,
His faith around her flew undone
And darkness hung the walls with baskets of snakes,
A furnace-nostrilled column-membered
Super-or-near man
Resembling to her dulled sense
The thief of adolescence,
Early imaginary half remembered
Oceanic lover alone
Jealousy cannot forget for all her sakes,
Made his bad bed in her good
Night, and enjoyed as he would.
Crying, white gowned, from the middle moonlit stages
Out to the tiered and hearing tide,
Close and far she announced the theft of the heart
In the taken body at many ages,
Trespasser and broken bride
Celebrating at her side
All blood-signed assailings and vanished marriages in which he
had no lovely part
Nor could share, for his pride, to the least
Mutter and foul wingbeat of the solemnizing nightpriest
Her holy unholy hours with the always anonymous beast.

(III)

Two sand grains together in bed,
Head to heaven-circling head,
Singly lie with the whole wide shore,
The covering sea their nightfall with no names;
And out of every domed and soil-based shell
One voice in chains declaims
The female, deadly, and male
Libidinous betrayal,
Golden dissolving under the water veil.
A she bird sleeping brittle by
Her lover's wings that fold tomorrow's flight,
Within the nested treefork
Sings to the treading hawk
Carrion, paradise, chirrup my bright yolk.
A blade of grass longs with the meadow,
A stone lies lost and locked in the lark-high hill.
Open as to the air to the naked shadow
O she lies alone and still,
Innocent between two wars,
With the incestuous secret brother in the seconds to perpetuate the stars,
A man torn up mourns in the sole night.
And the second comers, the severers, the enemies from the deep
Forgotten dark, rest their pulse and bury their dead in her faithless sleep.

Paper and Sticks

PAPER and sticks and shovel and match
Why won't the news of the old world catch
And the fire in a temper start

Once I had a rich boy for myself
I loved his body and his navy blue wealth
And I lived in his purse and his heart

When in our bed I was tossing and turning
All I could see were his brown eyes burning
By the green of a one pound note

I talk to him as I clean the grate
O my dear it 's never too late
To take me away as you whispered and wrote

I had a handsome and well-off boy
I 'll share my money and we 'll run for joy
With a bouncing and silver spooned kid

Sharp and shrill my silly tongue scratches
Words on the air as the fire catches
You never did and *he* never did.

Deaths and Entrances

On almost the incendiary eve
  Of several near deaths,
When one at the great least of your best loved
  And always known must leave
Lions and fires of his flying breath,
  Of your immortal friends
Who'd raise the organs of the counted dust
  To shoot and sing your praise,
One who called deepest down shall hold his peace
  That cannot sink or cease
  Endlessly to his wound
In many married London's estranging grief.

On almost the incendiary eve
  When at your lips and keys,
Locking, unlocking, the murdered strangers weave,
  One who is most unknown,
Your polestar neighbour, sun of another street,
  Will dive up to his tears.
He 'll bathe his raining blood in the male sea
  Who strode for your own dead
And wind his globe out of your water thread
  And load the throats of shells
  With every cry since light
Flashed first across his thunderclapping eyes.

On almost the incendiary eve
  Of deaths and entrances,
When near and strange wounded on London's waves

Have sought your single grave,
One enemy, of many, who knows well
Your heart is luminous
In the watched dark, quivering through locks and caves,
Will pull the thunderbolts
To shut the sun, plunge, mount your darkened keys
And sear just riders back,
Until that one loved least
Looms the last Samson of your zodiac.

A Winter's Tale

It is a winter's tale
That the snow blind twilight ferries over the lakes
And floating fields from the farm in the cup of the vales,
Gliding windless through the hand folded flakes,
The pale breath of cattle at the stealthy sail,

And the stars falling cold,
And the smell of hay in the snow, and the far owl
Warning among the folds, and the frozen hold
Flocked with the sheep white smoke of the farm house cowl
In the river wended vales where the tale was told.

Once when the world turned old
On a star of faith pure as the drifting bread,
As the food and flames of the snow, a man unrolled
The scrolls of fire that burned in his heart and head,
Torn and alone in a farm house in a fold

Of fields. And burning then
In his firelit island ringed by the winged snow
And the dung hills white as wool and the hen
Roosts sleeping chill till the flame of the cock crow
Combs through the mantled yards and the morning men

Stumble out with their spades,
The cattle stirring, the mousing cat stepping shy,
The puffed birds hopping and hunting, the milk maids
Gentle in their clogs over the fallen sky,
And all the woken farm at its white trades,

He knelt, he wept, he prayed,
By the spit and the black pot in the log bright light
And the cup and the cut bread in the dancing shade,
In the muffled house, in the quick of night,
At the point of love, forsaken and afraid.

He knelt on the cold stones,
He wept from the crest of grief, he prayed to the veiled sky
May his hunger go howling on bare white bones
Past the statues of the stables and the sky roofed sties
And the duck pond glass and the blinding byres alone

Into the home of prayers
And fires where he should prowl down the cloud
Of his snow blind love and rush in the white lairs.
His naked need struck him howling and bowed
Though no sound flowed down the hand folded air

But only the wind strung
Hunger of birds in the fields of the bread of water, tossed
In high corn and the harvest melting on their tongues.
And his nameless need bound him burning and lost
When cold as snow he should run the wended vales among

The rivers mouthed in night,
And drown in the drifts of his need, and lie curled caught
In the always desiring centre of the white
Inhuman cradle and the bride bed forever sought
By the believer lost and the hurled outcast of light.

Deliver him, he cried,
By losing him all in love, and cast his need
Alone and naked in the engulfing bride,
Never to flourish in the fields of the white seed
Or flower under the time dying flesh astride.

Listen. The minstrels sing
In the departed villages. The nightingale,
Dust in the buried wood, flies on the grains of her wings
And spells on the winds of the dead his winter's tale.
The voice of the dust of water from the withered spring

Is telling. The wizened
Stream with bells and baying water bounds. The dew rings
On the gristed leaves and the long gone glistening
Parish of snow. The carved mouths in the rock are wind
swept strings.
Time sings through the intricately dead snow drop. Listen.

It was a hand or sound
In the long ago land that glided the dark door wide
And there outside on the bread of the ground
A she bird rose and rayed like a burning bride.
A she bird dawned, and her breast with snow and scarlet
downed.

Look. And the dancers move
On the departed, snow bushed green, wanton in moon light
As a dust of pigeons. Exulting, the grave hooved
Horses, centaur dead, turn and tread the drenched white
Paddocks in the farms of birds. The dead oak walks for love.

The carved limbs in the rock
Leap, as to trumpets. Calligraphy of the old
Leaves is dancing. Lines of age on the stones weave in a flock.
And the harp shaped voice of the water's dust plucks in a fold
Of fields. For love, the long ago she bird rises. Look.

And the wild wings were raised
Above her folded head, and the soft feathered voice
Was flying through the house as though the she bird praised
And all the elements of the slow fall rejoiced
That a man knelt alone in the cup of the vales,

In the mantle and calm,
By the spit and the black pot in the log bright light.
And the sky of birds in the plumed voice charmed
Him up and he ran like a wind after the kindling flight
Past the blind barns and byres of the windless farm.

In the poles of the year
When black birds died like priests in the cloaked hedge row
And over the cloth of counties the far hills rode near,
Under the one leaved trees ran a scarecrow of snow
And fast through the drifts of the thickets antlered like deer,

Rags and prayers down the knee-
Deep hillocks and loud on the numbed lakes,
All night lost and long wading in the wake of the she-
Bird through the times and lands and tribes of the slow flakes.
Listen and look where she sails the goose plucked sea,

The sky, the bird, the bride,
The cloud, the need, the planted stars, the joy beyond
The fields of seed and the time dying flesh astride,
The heavens, the heaven, the grave, the burning font.
In the far ago land the door of his death glided wide,

And the bird descended.
On a bread white hill over the cupped farm
And the lakes and floating fields and the river wended
Vales where he prayed to come to the last harm
And the home of prayers and fires, the tale ended.

The dancing perishes
On the white, no longer growing green, and, minstrel dead,
The singing breaks in the snow shoed villages of wishes
That once cut the figures of birds on the deep bread
And over the glazed lakes skated the shapes of fishes

Flying. The rite is shorn
Of nightingale and centaur dead horse. The springs wither
Back. Lines of age sleep on the stones till trumpeting dawn.
Exultation lies down. Time buries the spring weather
That belled and bounded with the fossil and the dew reborn.

For the bird lay bedded
In a choir of wings, as though she slept or died,
And the wings glided wide and he was hymned and wedded,
And through the thighs of the engulfing bride,
The woman breasted and the heaven headed

Bird, he was brought low,
Burning in the bride bed of love, in the whirl-
Pool at the wanting centre, in the folds
Of paradise, in the spun bud of the world.
And she rose with him flowering in her melting snow.

On a Wedding Anniversary

THE sky is torn across
This ragged anniversary of two
Who moved for three years in tune
Down the long walks of their vows.

Now their love lies a loss
And Love and his patients roar on a chain;
From every true or crater
Carrying cloud, Death strikes their house.

Too late in the wrong rain
They come together whom their love parted:
The windows pour into their heart
And the doors burn in their brain.

There was a Saviour

THERE was a saviour
Rarer than radium,
Commoner than water, crueller than truth;
Children kept from the sun
Assembled at his tongue
To hear the golden note turn in a groove,
Prisoners of wishes locked their eyes
In the jails and studies of his keyless smiles.

The voice of children says
From a lost wilderness
There was calm to be done in his safe unrest,
When hindering man hurt
Man, animal, or bird
We hid our fears in that murdering breath,
Silence, silence to do, when earth grew loud,
In lairs and asylums of the tremendous shout.

There was glory to hear
In the churches of his tears,
Under his downy arm you sighed as he struck,
O you who could not cry
On to the ground when a man died
Put a tear for joy in the unearthly flood
And laid your cheek against a cloud-formed shell:
Now in the dark there is only yourself and myself.

Two proud, blacked brothers cry,
Winter-locked side by side,
To this inhospitable hollow year,
O we who could not stir
One lean sigh when we heard
Greed on man beating near and fire neighbour
But wailed and nested in the sky-blue wall
Now break a giant tear for the little known fall,

For the drooping of homes
That did not nurse our bones,
Brave deaths of only ones but never found,
Now see, alone in us,
Our own true strangers' dust
Ride through the doors of our unentered house.
Exiled in us we arouse the soft,
Unclenched, armless, silk and rough love that breaks
all rocks.

On the Marriage of a Virgin

WAKING alone in a multitude of loves when morning's light
Surprised in the opening of her nightlong eyes
His golden yesterday asleep upon the iris
And this day 's sun leapt up the sky out of her thighs
Was miraculous virginity old as loaves and fishes,
Though the moment of a miracle is unending lightning
And the shipyards of Galilee's footprints hide a navy of doves.

No longer will the vibrations of the sun desire on
Her deepsea pillow where once she married alone,
Her heart all ears and eyes, lips catching the avalanche
Of the golden ghost who ringed with his streams her mercury
    bone,
Who under the lids of her windows hoisted his golden luggage,
For a man sleeps where fire leapt down and she learns through
    his arm
That other sun, the jealous coursing of the unriva lled blood.

In my Craft or Sullen Art

IN my craft or sullen art
Exercised in the still night
When only the moon rages
And the lovers lie abed
With all their griefs in their arms,
I labour by singing light
Not for ambition or bread
Or the strut and trade of charms
On the ivory stages
But for the common wages
Of their most secret heart.

Not for the proud man apart
From the raging moon I write
On these spindrift pages
Nor for the towering dead
With their nightingales and psalms
But for the lovers, their arms
Round the griefs of the ages,
Who pay no praise or wages
Nor heed my craft or art.

Ceremony After a Fire Raid

(I)

MYSELVES
The grievers
Grieve
Among the street burned to tireless death
A child of a few hours
With its kneading mouth
Charred on the black breast of the grave
The mother dug, and its arms full of fires.

Begin
With singing
Sing
Darkness kindled back into beginning
When the caught tongue nodded blind,
A star was broken
Into the centuries of the child
Myselves grieve now, and miracles cannot atone.

Forgive
Us forgive
Us your death that myselves the believers
May hold it in a great flood
Till the blood shall spurt,
And the dust shall sing like a bird
As the grains blow, as your death grows, through
our heart.

Crying
Your dying
Cry,
Child beyond cockcrow, by the fire-dwarfed
Street we chant the flying sea
In the body bereft.
Love is the last light spoken. Oh
Seed of sons in the loin of the black husk left.

(II)

I know not whether
Adam or Eve, the adorned holy bullock
Or the white ewe lamb
Or the chosen virgin
Laid in her snow
On the altar of London,
Was the first to die
In the cinder of the little skull,
O bride and bride groom
O Adam and Eve together
Lying in the lull
Under the sad breast of the head stone
White as the skeleton
Of the garden of Eden.

I know the legend
Of Adam and Eve is never for a second
Silent in my service
Over the dead infants
Over the one

Child who was priest and servants,
Word, singers, and tongue
In the cinder of the little skull,
Who was the serpent's
Night fall and the fruit like a sun,
Man and woman undone,
Beginning crumbled back to darkness
Bare as the nurseries
Of the garden of wilderness.

(III)

Into the organpipes and steeples
Of the luminous cathedrals,
Into the weathercocks' molten mouths
Rippling in twelve-winded circles,
Into the dead clock burning the hour
Over the urn of sabbaths
Over the whirling ditch of daybreak
Over the sun's hovel and the slum of fire
And the golden pavements laid in requiems,
Into the bread in a wheatfield of flames,
Into the wine burning like brandy,
The masses of the sea
The masses of the sea under
The masses of the infant-bearing sea
Erupt, fountain, and enter to utter for ever
Glory glory glory
The sundering ultimate kingdom of genesis' thunder.

When I Woke

WHEN I woke, the town spoke.
Birds and clocks and cross bells
Dinned aside the coiling crowd,
The reptile profligates in a flame,
Spoilers and pokers of sleep,
The next-door sea dispelled
Frogs and satans and woman-luck,
While a man outside with a billhook,
Up to his head in his blood,
Cutting the morning off,
The warm-veined double of Time
And his scarving beard from a book,
Slashed down the last snake as though
It were a wand or subtle bough,
Its tongue peeled in the wrap of a leaf.

Every morning I make,
God in bed, good and bad,
After a water-face walk,
The death-stagged scatter-breath
Mammoth and sparrowfall
Everybody's earth.
Where birds ride like leaves and boats like ducks
I heard, this morning, waking,
Crossly out of the town noises
A voice in the erected air,
No prophet-progeny of mine,
Cry my sea town was breaking.
No Time, spoke the clocks, no God, rang the bells,
I drew the white sheet over the islands
And the coins on my eyelids sang like shells.

Among those Killed in the Dawn Raid was a Man Aged a Hundred

When the morning was waking over the war
He put on his clothes and stepped out and he died,
The locks yawned loose and a blast blew them wide,
He dropped where he loved on the burst pavement stone
And the funeral grains of the slaughtered floor.
Tell his street on its back he stopped a sun
And the craters of his eyes grew springshoots and fire
When all the keys shot from the locks, and rang.
Dig no more for the chains of his grey-haired heart.
The heavenly ambulance drawn by a wound
Assembling waits for the spade's ring on the cage.
O keep his bones away from that common cart,
The morning is flying on the wings of his age
And a hundred storks perch on the sun's right hand.

Lie Still, Sleep Becalmed

LIE still, sleep becalmed, sufferer with the wound
In the throat, burning and turning. All night afloat
On the silent sea we have heard the sound
That came from the wound wrapped in the salt sheet.

Under the mile off moon we trembled listening
To the sea sound flowing like blood from the loud wound
And when the salt sheet broke in a storm of singing
The voices of all the drowned swam on the wind.

Open a pathway through the slow sad sail,
Throw wide to the wind the gates of the wandering boat
For my voyage to begin to the end of my wound,
We heard the sea sound sing, we saw the salt sheet tell.
Lie still, sleep becalmed, hide the mouth in the throat,
Or we shall obey, and ride with you through the drowned.

Vision and Prayer

(1)

Who
Are you
Who is born
In the next room
So loud to my own
That I can hear the womb
Opening and the dark run
Over the ghost and the dropped son
Behind the wall thin as a wren's bone?
In the birth bloody room unknown
To the burn and turn of time
And the heart print of man
Bows no baptism
But dark alone
Blessing on
The wild
Child.

I
Must lie
Still as stone
By the wren bone
Wall hearing the moan
Of the mother hidden
And the shadowed head of pain
Casting tomorrow like a thorn
And the midwives of miracle sing
Until the turbulent new born
Burns me his name and his flame
And the winged wall is torn
By his torrid crown
And the dark thrown
From his loin
To bright
Light.

When
The wren
Bone writhes down
And the first dawn
Furied by his stream
Swarms on the kingdom come
Of the dazzler of heaven
And the splashed mothering maiden
Who bore him with a bonfire in
His mouth and rocked him like a storm
I shall run lost in sudden
Terror and shining from
The once hooded room
Crying in vain
In the caldron
Of his
Kiss

In
The spin
Of the sun
In the spuming
Cyclone of his wing
For I lost was who am
Crying at the man drenched throne
In the first fury of his stream
And the lightnings of adoration
Back to black silence melt and mourn
For I was lost who have come
To dumbfounding haven
And the finding one
And the high noon
Of his wound
Blinds my
Cry.

There
Crouched bare
In the shrine
Of his blazing
Breast I shall waken
To the judge blown bedlam
Of the uncaged sea bottom
The cloud climb of the exhaling tomb
And the bidden dust upsailing
With his flame in every grain.
O spiral of ascension
From the vultured urn
Of the morning
Of man when
The land
And

The

Born sea

Praised the sun

The finding one

And upright Adam

Sang upon origin!

O the wings of the children!

The woundward flight of the ancient

Young from the canyons of oblivion!

The sky stride of the always slain

In battle! the happening

Of saints to their vision!

The world winding home!

And the whole pain

Flows open

And I

Die.

(II)

In the name of the lost who glory in
The swinish plains of carrion
Under the burial song
Of the birds of burden
Heavy with the drowned
And the green dust
And bearing
The ghost
From
The ground
Like pollen
On the black plume
And the beak of slime
I pray though I belong
Not wholly to that lamenting
Brethren for joy has moved within
The inmost marrow of my heart bone

That he who learns now the sun and moon
Of his mother's milk may return
Before the lips blaze and bloom
To the birth bloody room
Behind the wall's wren
Bone and be dumb
And the womb
That bore
For
All men
The adored
Infant light or
The dazzling prison
Yawn to his upcoming.
In the name of the wanton
Lost on the unchristened mountain
In the centre of dark I pray him

Then he let the dead lie though they moan
For his briared hands to hoist them
To the shrine of his world's wound
And the blood drop's garden
Endure the stone
Blind host to sleep
In the dark
And deep
Rock
Awake
No heart bone
But let it break
On the mountain crown
Unbidden by the sun
And the beating dust be blown
Down to the river rooting plain
Under the night forever falling.

Forever falling night is a known
Star and country to the legion
Of sleepers whose tongue I toll
To mourn his deluging
Light through sea and soil
And we have come
To know all
Places
Ways
Mazes
Passages
Quarters and graves
Of the endless fall.
Now common lazarus
Of the charting sleepers prays
Never to awake and arise
For the country of death is the heart's size

And the star of the lost the shape of the eyes.
In the name of the fatherless
In the name of the unborn
And the undesirers
Of midwiving morning's
Hands or instruments
O in the name
Of no one
Now or
No
One to
Be I pray
May the crimson
Sun spin a grave grey
And the colour of clay
Stream upon his martyrdom
In the interpreted evening
And the known dark of the earth amen.

I turn the corner of prayer and burn
In a blessing of the sudden
Sun. In the name of the damned
I would turn back and run
To the hidden land
But the loud sun
Christens down
The sky.
I
Am found.
O let him
Scald me and drown
Me in his world's wound.
His lightning answers my
Cry. My voice burns in his hand.
Now I am lost in the blinding
One. The sun roars at the prayer's end.

Ballad of the Long-legged Bait

THE bows glided down, and the coast
Blackened with birds took a last look
At his thrashing hair and whale-blue eye;
The trodden town rang its cobbles for luck.

Then goodbye to the fishermanned
Boat with its anchor free and fast
As a bird hooking over the sea,
High and dry by the top of the mast,

Whispered the affectionate sand
And the bulwarks of the dazzled quay.
For my sake sail, and never look back,
Said the looking land.

Sails drank the wind, and white as milk
He sped into the drinking dark;
The sun shipwrecked west on a pearl
And the moon swam out of its hulk.

Funnels and masts went by in a whirl.
Goodbye to the man on the sea-legged deck
To the gold gut that sings on his reel
To the bait that stalked out of the sack,

For we saw him throw to the swift flood
A girl alive with his hooks through her lips;
All the fishes were rayed in blood,
Said the dwindling ships.

Goodbye to chimneys and funnels,
Old wives that spin in the smoke,
He was blind to the eyes of candles
In the praying windows of waves

But heard his bait buck in the wake
And tussle in a shoal of loves.
Now cast down your rod, for the whole
Of the sea is hilly with whales,

She longs among horses and angels,
The rainbow-fish bend in her joys,
Floated the lost cathedral
Chimes of the rocked buoys.

Where the anchor rode like a gull
Miles over the moonstruck boat
A squall of birds bellowed and fell,
A cloud blew the rain from its throat;

He saw the storm smoke out to kill
With fuming bows and ram of ice,
Fire on starlight, rake Jesu's stream;
And nothing shone on the water's face

But the oil and bubble of the moon,
Plunging and piercing in his course
The lured fish under the foam
Witnessed with a kiss.

Whales in the wake like capes and Alps
Quaked the sick sea and snouted deep,
Deep the great bushed bait with raining lips
Slipped the fins of those humpbacked tons

And fled their love in a weaving dip.
Oh, Jericho was falling in their lungs!
She nipped and dived in the nick of love,
Spun on a spout like a long-legged ball

Till every beast blared down in a swerve
Till every turtle crushed from his shell
Till every bone in the rushing grave
Rose and crowed and fell!

Good luck to the hand on the rod,
There is thunder under its thumbs;
Gold gut is a lightning thread,
His fiery reel sings off its flames,

The whirled boat in the burn of his blood
Is crying from nets to knives,
Oh the shearwater birds and their boatsized brood
Oh the bulls of Biscay and their calves

Are making under the green, laid veil
The long-legged beautiful bait their wives.
Break the black news and paint on a sail
Huge weddings in the waves,

Over the wakeward-flashing spray
Over the gardens of the floor
Clash out the mounting dolphin's day,
My mast is a bell-spire,

Strike and smoothe, for my decks are drums,
Sing through the water-spoken prow
The octopus walking into her limbs
The polar eagle with his tread of snow.

From salt-lipped beak to the kick of the stern
Sing how the seal has kissed her dead!
The long, laid minute's bride drifts on
Old in her cruel bed.

Over the graveyard in the water
Mountains and galleries beneath
Nightingale and hyena
Rejoicing for that drifting death

Sing and howl through sand and anemone
Valley and sahara in a shell,
Oh all the wanting flesh his enemy
Thrown to the sea in the shell of a girl

Is old as water and plain as an eel;
Always goodbye to the long-legged bread
Scattered in the paths of his heels
For the salty birds fluttered and fed

And the tall grains foamed in their bills;
Always goodbye to the fires of the face,
For the crab-backed dead on the sea-bed rose
And scuttled over her eyes,

The blind, clawed stare is cold as sleet.
The tempter under the eyelid
Who shows to the selves asleep
Mast-high moon-white women naked

Walking in wishes and lovely for shame
Is dumb and gone with his flame of brides.
Sussanah's drowned in the bearded stream
And no-one stirs at Sheba's side

But the hungry kings of the tides;
Sin who had a woman's shape
Sleeps till Silence blows on a cloud
And all the lifted waters walk and leap.

Lucifer that bird's dropping
Out of the sides of the north
Has melted away and is lost
Is always lost in her vaulted breath,

Venus lies star-struck in her wound
And the sensual ruins make
Seasons over the liquid world,
White springs in the dark.

Always goodbye, cried the voices through the shell,
Goodbye always for the flesh is cast
And the fisherman winds his reel
With no more desire than a ghost.

Always good luck, praised the finned in the feather
Bird after dark and the laughing fish
As the sails drank up the hail of thunder
And the long-tailed lightning lit his catch.

The boat swims into the six-year weather,
A wind throws a shadow and it freezes fast.
See what the gold gut drags from under
Mountains and galleries to the crest!

See what clings to hair and skull
As the boat skims on with drinking wings!
The statues of great rain stand still,
And the flakes fall like hills.

Sing and strike his heavy haul
Toppling up the boatside in a snow of light!
His decks are drenched with miracles.
Oh miracle of fishes! The long dead bite!

Out of the urn the size of a man
Out of the room the weight of his trouble
Out of the house that holds a town
In the continent of a fossil

One by one in dust and shawl,
Dry as echoes and insect-faced,
His fathers cling to the hand of the girl
And the dead hand leads the past,

Leads them as children and as air
On to the blindly tossing tops;
The centuries throw back their hair
And the old men sing from newborn lips:

Time is bearing another son.
Kill Time! She turns in her pain!
The oak is felled in the acorn
And the hawk in the egg kills the wren.

He who blew the great fire in
And died on a hiss of flames
Or walked on the earth in the evening
Counting the denials of the grains

Clings to her drifting hair, and climbs;
And he who taught their lips to sing
Weeps like the risen sun among
The liquid choirs of his tribes.

The rod bends low, divining land,
And through the sundered water crawls
A garden holding to her hand
With birds and animals

With men and women and waterfalls
Trees cool and dry in the whirlpool of ships
And stunned and still on the green, laid veil
Sand with legends in its virgin laps

And prophets loud on the burned dunes;
Insects and valleys hold her thighs hard,
Time and places grip her breast bone,
She is breaking with seasons and clouds;

Round her trailed wrist fresh water weaves,
With moving fish and rounded stones
Up and down the greater waves
A separate river breathes and runs;

Strike and sing his catch of fields
For the surge is sown with barley,
The cattle graze on the covered foam,
The hills have footed the waves away,

With wild sea fillies and soaking bridles
With salty colts and gales in their limbs
All the horses of his haul of miracles
Gallop through the arched, green farms,

Trot and gallop with gulls upon them
And thunderbolts in their manes.
O Rome and Sodom Tomorrow and London
The country tide is cobbled with towns,

And steeples pierce the cloud on her shoulder
And the streets that the fisherman combed
When his long-legged flesh was a wind on fire
And his loin was a hunting flame

Coil from the thoroughfares of her hair
And terribly lead him home alive
Lead her prodigal home to his terror,
The furious ox-killing house of love.

Down, down, down, under the ground,
Under the floating villages,
Turns the moon-chained and water-wound
Metropolis of fishes,

There is nothing left of the sea but its sound,
Under the earth the loud sea walks,
In deathbeds of orchards the boat dies down
And the bait is drowned among hayricks,

Land, land, land, nothing remains
Of the pacing, famous sea but its speech,
And into its talkative seven tombs
The anchor dives through the floors of a church.

Goodbye, good luck, struck the sun and the moon,
To the fisherman lost on the land.
He stands alone at the door of his home,
With his long-legged heart in his hand.

Holy Spring

O
Out of a bed of love
When that immortal hospital made one more move to soothe
The cureless counted body,
And ruin and his causes
Over the barbed and shooting sea assumed an army
And swept into our wounds and houses,
I climb to greet the war in which I have no heart but only
That one dark I owe my light,
Call for confessor and wiser mirror but there is none
To glow after the god stoning night
And I am struck as lonely as a holy maker by the sun.

No
Praise that the spring time is all
Gabriel and radiant shrubbery as the morning grows joyful
Out of the woebegone pyre
And the multitude's sultry tear turns cool on the weeping wall,
My arising prodigal
Sun the father his quiver full of the infants of pure fire,
But blessed be hail and upheaval
That uncalm still it is sure alone to stand and sing
Alone in the husk of man's home
And the mother and toppling house of the holy spring,
If only for a last time.

Fern Hill

Now as I was young and easy under the apple boughs
About the lilting house and happy as the grass was green,
    The night above the dingle starry,
        Time let me hail and climb
    Golden in the heydays of his eyes,
And honoured among wagons I was prince of the apple towns
And once below a time I lordly had the trees and leaves
        Trail with daisies and barley
    Down the rivers of the windfall light.

And as I was green and carefree, famous among the barns
About the happy yard and singing as the farm was home,
    In the sun that is young once only,
        Time let me play and be
    Golden in the mercy of his means,
And green and golden I was huntsman and herdsman, the calves
Sang to my horn, the foxes on the hills barked clear and cold,
        And the sabbath rang slowly
    In the pebbles of the holy streams.

All the sun long it was running, it was lovely, the hay
Fields high as the house, the tunes from the chimneys, it was air
    And playing, lovely and watery
        And fire green as grass.
    And nightly under the simple stars
As I rode to sleep the owls were bearing the farm away,
All the moon long I heard, blessed among stables, the nightjars
    Flying with the ricks, and the horses
        Flashing into the dark.

And then to awake, and the farm, like a wanderer white
With the dew, come back, the cock on his shoulder; it was all
Shining, it was Adam and maiden,
The sky gathered again
And the sun grew round that very day.
So it must have been after the birth of the simple light
In the first, spinning place, the spellbound horses walking warm
Out of the whinnying green stable
On to the fields of praise.

And honoured among foxes and pheasants by the gay house
Under the new made clouds and happy as the heart was long,
In the sun born over and over,
I ran my heedless ways,
My wishes raced through the house high hay
And nothing I cared, at my sky blue trades, that time allows
In all his tuneful turning so few and such morning songs
Before the children green and golden
Follow him out of grace,

Nothing I cared, in the lamb white days, that time would take me
Up to the swallow thronged loft by the shadow of my hand,
In the moon that is always rising,
Nor that riding to sleep
I should hear him fly with the high fields
And wake to the farm forever fled from the childless land.
Oh as I was young and easy in the mercy of his means,
Time held me green and dying
Though I sang in my chains like the sea.